# Ashes To Life

# Ashes To Life

*A Book of Story-Poems*
*of life emerging from the embers of ashes*

O. Virginia Phillips, Ph.D.

The Family Connection Publications

FIRST EDITION
1st Printing, November, 1994

Library of Congress Catalog Card Number: 94-094337

ISBN: 0-9641507-0-0

Printed in The United States of America
by Barclay Press, Newberg, Oregon

Illustrations by Rondahl A. Mitchell-Phillips


For information address:
The Family Connection Publications
P.O. Box 796, Newberg, Oregon, 97132

# Contents

# Acknowledgments

My special gratitude to Mary Myton, for her honest critique, typing, formatting and her burden bearing spirit as she has stood with me these many years. My appreciation to Joshua, my husband, friend and mentor who daily encourages me in my many pursuits, and to Mikki Snell who continues to be excited about the poems and their possibilities.

# ∼· Preface ·∼

It was lonely the morning these stories literally spilled over from my memory into written words. I was in Battle Creek, Michigan without my family and friends. The ashes of loneliness would have enveloped me, but as I meditated I saw the lives of persons that I knew who were touched in their moments of ashes by a life-impacting resource and my loneliness lifted. I reached for the pen waiting by my bedside and began to encourage myself. This occurred each morning for thirteen days and then I put my pen down. Months later, I reread these story-poems and invited others to read them. I knew then as I know now, that they are meant to encourage others wherever this book will alight.

These individuals found life through an impartation of the human spirit given by the supernatural resources of God.

# ~· How Can I Dance?

# Robert ⌣·

We moved to California when I was eight. My good memories were those of living with Grandmother in North Carolina — Sunday pot-lucks on the grass, dancing before the Lord in the little white Pentecostal church, talking, singing, visiting all day on the church grounds. I'm nineteen now.

## Ashes

Some folks say I got rhythm,
— and they expect me to dance.
Just because I'm black
        — I'm expected to prance.

When I was younger I felt like dancin',
things didn't bother me the way they do now.
When I was in the country,
        I was happier somehow.

Then we moved to the city,
amongst the noise and concrete.
I can't hear birds sing, see rabbits run
        or hear crickets creak.

I'd go back south
if I had my say.
There ain't nothing here for me,
        I've lost my way.

If I could I'd leave here
'cause most days I'm in a trance.
Yeh, in my younger days down south
        I really did dance!

How can I dance on concrete
with broken glass,
jagged sidewalks
        and such?

Here where I live,
dancin'
don't mean
        that much.  ⌣·

## Life ~·

I passed that little white church for years,
        it sits on the corner of Russell and Spears.
Across the street was Mr. Cool's,
        a honkey-tonk joint where I go to play pool.

That little church attracted me so,
        whenever I passed it, I'd walk real slow.
Sometimes I'd listen to the shouting inside,
        and the struggle inside me seemed to subside.

Sometime I'd peek in the side window,
        hoping by chance
It would be the time
        for those old sisters to dance.

What a sight to see,
        they could both twirl and shout,
Even the noise at Mr. Cool's
        couldn't drown them out.

My weekly routine brought me in touch
        with the emotional expression I needed so much.
It reminded me of my grandmother's old church down south,
        where we spent all day Sunday in sweet fellowship.

I remember how proud the old ladies were
        when I would sing a song;
Those were the good old days,
        when I could do no wrong.

I passed that little church again,
        this time I stopped and went in.
After the first time visiting,
        I went again and again.

I found something there,
        I've made a new start.
Dancin's not just in my feet,
        it's deep in my heart. ~·

~· **How Can I Love?**

# Tony

I used to live with my mother and her boyfriend. They spent their time partying and drinking. Most of the time I felt invisible because I was afraid if I spoke I would stutter and my mother would slap me. I really wanted to touch or hug my mother, but I couldn't. Things are different now, I am with Miz Sadie.

## Ashes

I daydream a lot
'cause
everything around me hurts.

My mom says I'm dumb,
and
her boyfriend thinks I'm a curse.

I don't talk much
'cause
nothing I say makes much sense.

I get so scared when I try
to speak—
the slaps across my mouth hurt so bad.

I wonder why Momma had me.
She
never wanted me, she said.

Sometimes, when I am alone
I think
I'd be better off dead.

Why stay in a place
where
nobody feels or touches.

I feel like a cripple
scared
without any crutches.

I dream of falling,
but
I never land.

There is a silent yell inside
                that I
try to voice, and never can.

Miz Sadie down the street
                stops
sometimes to talk to me.

Whenever I pass her corner,
                she says
"Jesus loves you,  you can be free."

I don't understand what she means,
                but
when she looks at me

I see in her eyes, something
                is different
from my mother's stare.

And she talks to me
                about
love,  faith and prayer.

I want this love she speaks about,
                but
I pretend I don't care.

She says "come to church"
                but
I don't dare —

They might think I'm dumb
                like
My Momma does.

I am curious though
about
how it feels to be loved.

I want to know
inside
how can I love?  ～·

## *Life*

When Miz Sadie touches—as she often does,
    A body feels warm, comforted and loved.
She does it when I don't expect her to,
    Most likely it's when I'm feeling blue.

It just comes natural,
    Miz Sadie's touch.
I wish I could live with Miz Sadie,
    I need her so much.

Today they took my Momma away,
    I cried 'cause I had no place to stay.
But Miz Sadie came and took me home,
    She touched me and hugged me and called me her own.

Finally I'm beginning to believe there is a God above,
    Like Miz Sadie says—I can learn to love.
'Cause the scream inside me is no longer there,
    I feel real good—I belong somewhere.

# How Can I Sing?

# Linda ⌣·

Here I am twenty-six years old and a single mother. I have five children. I have this desire to sing, sometimes it's overwhelming. I often think about a nice home, a car, a good job and singing. The singing brings back memories of the times I sang in the Junior Choir at church; I was happy then. These days it seems like I ain't got no song. I need to make some choices.

## Ashes

How can I sing
when I got no job
and no self-esteem? Anyway,
people with good voices sing. People
who have money, live in fine neighborhoods and
wear diamond rings sing.

Rich folks can sing, shing-a ling,
buy fine cars,
and do everything.
People like that
can afford to sing.
I ain't got those things, I can't sing.

How can I sing?
Me, who lives in a dump
has a house full of kids,
and feels like a frump —
I want a proper house;
until then I can't sing.

I won't sing a song
I don't even feel,
make up a tune that
just ain't real.
Until I get that tune I can't sing.

The problem is
I ain't got
no song.
Something in my life went wrong
How can I sing?

## Life ⌣·

A quiet rhythm evolves in my soul
      when I look straight into my pain.
I begin to hum, to cheer myself and
      out comes a simple refrain.

Nothing brilliant —you understand, but
      something I can control.
It takes me away from the daily heartache
      that can so easily take hold.

Somewhere I recall something I read,
      it was on a neighborhood sign:
"Anything in life is possible,
      it first begins in your mind."

No one knows what's in my mind,
      I can think anything right or wrong.
The choice is mine at any time,
      I can even think up a song.

I can choose to sing, dress like a queen,
      dream big dreams in my head.
My mind I can control whenever I choose,
      no need to be afraid.

A sweet refrain wells up in my soul,
      today can be a brighter day.
I CAN SING, the choice is mine.
      A song can just happen that way. ⌣·

~· *How Can I Care?*

# Betty Jo ~·

I am married and my husband works part-time because he is in school. I had to care for my younger sister and brother when I was growing up and I vowed never to have children. Yet here I am with a full-time job and two children. I have been hearing a lot lately about caring and I think to myself, I can hardly handle my own problems, how can I take on the cares of others? I am simply too busy to care for other folks.

# Ashes ⌣·

What am I supposed to do
about the folks down the street?
I have enough to do just to keep the peace
in my own house:
>        thinking about the bills,
>        the boss at work
>        washing clothes
>        and ironing shirts.

Then I go to church to get some ease,
"care for your neighbors" — Oh, please!
They don't care for themselves...
>        daughter pregnant again,
>        and the boy's on dope.
They could better themselves;
they don't need no strokes.

As hard as I work, I ain't got time
to wine and dine
folks in their prime.
Where's everyone when I need
>        a helping hand sometimes?
>        I have too little time to spare.
How can I take time to care? ⌣·

# Life ⌁·

"Betty Jo, come in here
    and see to your sister Lynn."
I can hear my Momma's voice now,
    as clearly as I did then.

Lynn was one and I was five.
    Her diapers were never clean.
I hated to stop in the middle of play,
    to hear my sister scream.

Whenever I cleaned her dirty behind
    she yelled 'cause I stuck her with the pin.
Then Momma would call out, "Betty Jo,
    what in the world are you doing to Lynn?"

Momma was always busy,
    but she had time to spare.
She rocked us on her soft warm lap
    in her old creaky rocking chair.

She told us stories of her own childhood
    when her mother was alive and well.
Grannie raised seventeen children, only five were hers,
    and she had many stories to tell.

Momma remembered what Grannie taught
    and passed it along to me,
"Plant a seed of love and care,
    you'll reap plenty to share."

When I take time to remember
    the life Momma lived each day,
a part of her is alive in me —
    I can take time to care. ⌁·

How Can I Cry?

# Ron ⌣·

Big Mama left me unprotected and afraid, how could she leave me in such despair? How could she die on me like that? I thought she would live forever, she was so strong and full of faith. I want to cry, but the pain gets in the way.

## Ashes

Big Mamma died yesterday.
She was the key that opened my heart to sing,
              — but she left me.

Big Mamma talked to me when I was sad,
laughed with me when I was glad,
              — but she left me.

Big Mamma cared for me when I was born,
the only parent I have ever known,
              — but she left me.

Big Mamma listened when Mother wouldn't
and Father couldn't,
              — but she left me.

Big Mamma protected me from the streets,
taught me the meaning of freedom,
              — but she left me.

Now I stand and watch them take her away,
a lingering ache that just won't break,
              — Big Mamma left me.

The people around me weep, my hearts says try,
but I can't cry,
              — Big Mamma left me.

There is no one to hold me, love me, console me.
How can I cry?
              — Big Mamma left me.

## Life ~·

Something inside me reminds me of Sundays
when Big Mamma took me to church.
"Boy, you got to always pray
      and don't let yourself fall by the way,"

"We are born and we will die,
      life ain't no pie in the sky,"
"You got to remember when to work and when to play,
      when to laugh and when to cry,"

"While the world is in a spin,
      take the time to look within,"
"There you will find strength,
      purpose and Peace."

"Whatever you hold that hurts,
      you've got to release,"
"Cause everything will pass
      and people will change by and by,"

"It's all right to cry when something hurts,
      tears wash away the pain,"
"When the flowing stops, put your hand to the plow,
      your living is not in vain,"

I think on those things Big Mamma would say,
      and the tears begin to flow.
She is here with me as she always will be,
      gently prodding me as I go.

Whenever I get lost and can't find my way,
      I remember what Big Mamma would say.
And when my heart is overwhelmed
      I find a quiet place and cry. ~·

# How Can I Be Faithful?

# Joseph ⌁·

Faithful wasn't a way of life for my Uncle Tim. He taught me well that one woman wasn't enough. Although it pained me to see my Auntie Joy hurt from my Uncle Tim's escapades with other women, I grew up thinking Uncle Tim's way must have been acceptable. I learned a different lesson when I met Thomas Farr.

## Ashes

I grew up in a big old house
with Grandma, three aunts, two cousins
             and Uncle Tim.
Since I was the only boy, Uncle Tim told me
I could hang around with him.
             Uncle Tim was
married to Auntie Joy,
who treated me special,
             she called me her little man.
It was understood that Uncle Tim
would teach me what boys should know,
             that was the plan.
I learned a lot from Uncle Tim,
how to shoot marbles, ride a bike
             and cop a plea.
But my greatest love was Auntie Joy,
she was mighty
             good to me.
I looked up to Uncle Tim
and believed everything he did
             was right,
even when he took me to the corner joint,
where he drank until the
             middle of the night.
He told me to tell Auntie Joy
that he was playing cards with the boys,
             that made me feel bad.
But Uncle Tim said it was o.k.
'cause if I told the truth,
             Auntie Joy would be sad.
Pretty soon the hurt from the lies
grew duller and duller,
             as I followed Uncle Tim.

Even when he began to take me
to visit his lady friend
                    named Aunt Em.
I really didn't want to go.
I didn't even want to know what happened
                    when he sent me outside to play.
Once I asked Uncle Tim
how Auntie Joy would feel and he said,
        " Life is just that way."
Those things haunted me as I grew,
I knew something
                    was not right.
But when I became a man
childish thoughts
                    took flight.
One woman just don't seem to be enough
to satisfy
                    my needs.
"Settle down,
stop running around,"
                    something inside me pleads.
My thoughts
often turn
                    to Auntie Joy.
I want to be faithful —
and then I remember
                    my life as a boy.
How can I be faithful? ⌣·

## Life ~·

I finally moved to a house 'way across town.
I noticed an old gentleman watching me,
     who lived two doors down.
One day he walked up as I was getting out of my car.
He held out his hand and said, " Welcome,
     my name is Thomas Farr.
I am your neighbor,
and anything you need
     I'd be glad to oblige."
That old man was tall and straight
with kind and gentle eyes.
     His hands were strong,
and when he smiled, it furrowed his brow.
He reminded me of Uncle Tim,
     but he was different somehow.

As the days went by I began to visit,
he took care of his wife who was an invalid —
     she was the pride of his life.
I couldn't understand how he could be so tender,
he never raised his voice when he spoke,
     his speech was kind and gentle.
Listening to him talk and watching his life
     gave me the strength to seek out a wife.
Because of Thomas Farr, I learned a valuable lesson:
to be a faithful and loving to one woman
     is a lifelong blessing.
I can be faithful. ~·

*How Can I Speak?*

# J.T. ⌣

I never felt that my
words meant anything;
no one listened and my
language was never good enough
for the teachers. Things are
different now.

  — someone came to listen —

Say what, speak?
Speak on what? What will I say?
I can't even understand the language today.

## Ashes ~·

When I go to school,
I'm expected to learn.
I ain't even ate, but that's nobody's concern.

My old man don't work,
My mom makes just enough
to pay the rent and the light bill. Man its tough!

When I get to school
the teacher expects me to read.
So much going on in the room nobody pays any heed.

Why should I speak
nobody listens,
'cept James and Jamar, Pop Man and Christen.

They all understand
'cause they's
in the same condition.

Speak, you say,
let me tell you the situation.
My language ain't even accepted.

The teacher don't care —
she's too busy belittling me.
In order to speak you need to feel safe.

The stuff they teach ain't about me,
where I live or what I do.
How can I speak? ~·

# Life ～·

A lady came by our house today.
she works in the 'hood, her name is Miss Fay.
She asked me what I liked to do.
I didn't understand what she was referring to.

She told me they were doing some kind of survey
to find out what people had to say
about where they live, their schools and even their sidewalks.
Before I knew it, I began to talk.

I told her everything I could think about,
my voice grew louder, I began to shout!
I shook my head, waved my hands and I could see
the lady was really listening to me.

She was interested in what I had to say
about the place I lived in day after day.
I surprised myself. I felt so good
speaking about things that happen in my neighborhood.

I began to understand what was missing —
all I needed was someone to listen!
For once in my life I started to believe
in me — I can speak. ～·

*How Can I Touch?*

# Bonita ⌣·

Just a single touch is all
I need to get by. My soul
screams for it, my heart beats
for it and my body aches for it.

## Ashes

How can I touch when there ain't so much
as a real friend I can call my own?
I walk around town feeling like a clown,
meeting people on the street, at the beauty parlor,
lollygagging, pretending, trying to make a dollar.
"Hey girlfriend," I hear, but I kno' she ain't my friend.
She's just repeating those words to fit in.
These are trying times,
           time without love,
                      time without hope.
Sometimes I try to hug my ol' man
but he's at the end of his rope,
nobody cares anymore,
everybody doing their own thing.
My soul is screaming,
I need to touch — somebody.
           How can I touch
                      when nobody touches me?

## Life ~·

" Come on in, Bonita, sit down and rest."
(She actually remembered my name!)
This was the third time I visited
      and the greeting was still the same.
I could not believe
      she would even invite me in.
This lady hardly knew me,
      yet she acted like a friend.

I knocked on her door one day
out of curiosity.
Some girls who stayed with her
      were once as bad off as me.
Some of them were former prostitutes
      and members of gangs.
But after a few months with this lady,
      they suddenly changed.

I was so down one day,
I could hardly see
Roberta (one of the other girls) said,
      "Come home with me."
I thought she was lying
      so I didn't go.
Then the next day I got enough nerve
      to knock on the door.

From the very first visit
something happened inside me.
I returned again and again
      to check my reality.

I didn't talk at first,
  she knew how I felt.
It was strange at first
  'cause I didn't know myself.

There was so much locked up inside of me.
One day she said,
" Bonita, you need to be free
  of bitterness, hatred and pain.
Holding it inside
  will only drive you insane."

She began to talk to me,
her words were gentle and feeling.
She accepted me as I was,
  which brought about my healing.
It took a long time
  and many, many visits.
She never turned me away,
  no matter how busy.

She was always ready to listen
to someone like me.
This lady knew how to touch
  a broken heart and set it free.
I can touch now —
  because she touched me.

## How Can I Laugh?

# Omar ⁓·

I hang out a lot on the
corner, there's nobody at
home to talk with.
At least on the corner there
are people…

## Ashes

Ah'm always grinning. Can't you see?
    I holler loud
        at a good joke
            that tickles me.

I can show some teeth
    and tell some puns,
        I can keep folk screaming
            and having fun.

The guys on the corner
    love to see me coming,
        they gather around
            to hear something funny.

I entertain for hours
    starting early in the morning —
        from dusk to dawn
            Ah'm having fun.

'Cause there's nothing else to do
    and no other place to go
        'cept wait for some weed I can't afford —
            at least it keeps me from being bored.

In a few minutes I forget
    that I severed the cord
        of reality, creativity
            and possibility.

Grinning
    and laughing,
        but nobody sees
            the pain.

## *Life*

" Hey Omar! Man, what you doing? Getting married?
You ain't got no money,
and that ol' piecy job you  got
don't pay no salary..."
>I didn't listen to the rest
>of what Jarell had to say.
>My heart is pounding
>Ah'm tieing the knot today.

It didn't seem real,
I was walking in a dream —
it began twelve months ago
when I met Emogene.
>I was working at a center
>and she was there, too.
>As usual, I told a joke,
>but I didn't have a clue.

Emogene would actually listen
and encourage more.
She really laughed at my jokes
and my hungry heart soared.
>She was so easy to talk to
>and her smile lit up the room.
>She walked with such pride,
>everything about her was groomed.

Emogene became the center
of my reality.
She taught me the meaning
of creativity and possibility.

She told me over and over
that I could succeed.
With the talent I have
I didn't need weed.

Now I finally laugh!
        It feels so right.
Emogene has helped me
        sort out my life.

My life has meaning;
        I took the risk
        to let Emogene look inside me,
I can live not simply exist.
I can laugh. ⌣·

# How Can I Play?

# Jason ⌣·

I am one of Mr. Casey's kids.
Mr. Casey operates a community center in L.A.
His kids call him "Mr T." for "tenacious."

## Ashes ⌣

You say "play." I ain't got no decent toys.
Kids on TV have toys,
all kinds,
even ones that make noise.

I want to play outside,
but I can't go to the park.
      B.J., he's standing on the corner ready to take me apart.
He wants my jacket
      my grandmother bought.
If I go play basketball,
      I might get caught.

How can I play, anyway?
I'm just day dreaming about the day
when I can walk down the street
      and feel okay.

Who plays nowadays?
Tell me!
      How can I play? ⌣

# Life ~·

Mr. Casey knocked hard,
      but I didn't answer.
It didn't seem to discourage him —
      he just knocked harder.
Finally, during a TV commercial
      I heard him call,
"Anybody home? It's cold
      here in this hall."

It was only twenty degrees outside,
      and the hallway wasn't heated.
In the projects, even some of the
      walls weren't completed.
I huddle up in the winter time and watch TV
      until late at night when I can hardly see.
It's better than going outside
      and getting my head bashed in.
      Unless I join the neighborhood gang,
      I won't have a friend.

Mr. Casey's been coming around lately
      talking to me.
He directs a new program
      that he wants me to see.
I've been avoiding him
      'cause I don't believe
nobody's program
      will change the way I live.

He said, "If you come and don't like it,
        I'll bring you right home."
I finally said, "Okay, okay, I'll come."
        I thought to myself,
"How can a nice guy like him
        be so dumb?
Doesn't he know the kids around here
        play with guns?"

Well, I followed him outside
        to his waiting van.
It was practically full of guys,
        they all yelled, "Hey, man!"
As I ventured inside and took a seat
        the guy next to me smiled
and gave me a five hand.
        It was neat.

When we got to the building —
        I was really surprised.
It was only nine blocks away,
        but it was clean and nice.
There were a lot of other kids there
        just about my age.
They waved and greeted me,
        *Oh wow! what a place!*

There was a section with books, some desks,
      a music room and plenty more.
I even saw a game room
      as I continued to explore.
I saw some guys that
      lived in my building.

They were playing basketball.
      I yelled, "Hey man hey!"
      At last I found a place
      where it's safe to play.

~· *How Can I Whisper?*

# Jeanine ‿·

Inside of me there is
such a storm, even if
I whisper it's too loud.
The pain inside is one
long scream I want
out, but I am too scared
to leave this
ache I am so accustomed to.

# Ashes ◡·

How can I whisper
when inside I'm screaming for life?
The darkness around me is so great
I can see no light.
                              I yell!

The noise makes me feel there is
some one there
beside me.
I wonder – can anyone hear
                              my heart beat?

Feeling neglected
and full of despair.
I am afraid to be quiet.
The vast quietness will declare
                              my loneliness.

I cannot whisper, I yell!
The sound reverberates
loud, crisp and clear.
I imagine someone else
                              is near.

How can I whisper?
I am afraid of what I might hear.
Deep in my soul
is my worst fear
                              I am alone. ◡·

## Life

I don't know how he found me.
  For so long I have felt invisible.
  All I feel is pain, my life is miserable.
  The kind of pain no one can fix.
  When it gets too bad, I turn some tricks.

For a little while I don't feel alone.
  Someone is holding me, I pretend I'm loved.
  I can't explain my feeling to anyone.
  All I know is I need someone
  to fill this empty void.

People think I enjoy selling my body.
  Most of the time I just give it away —
  it makes up for the love I never had.
  I feel empty, vulnerable —
  an easy prey.

My mother's 'ol man raped me when I was six, I knew it was wrong.
  It happened so often, no one listened.
  I have lived this way too long —
  talking loud, keeping a grin on my face.
  I felt like killing myself the day Rev. J. came to my place.

He had kind eyes and a gentle smile.
  He asked me if he could talk to me a while.
  I thought "I can use the company," so I said, "Fine."
  I had never met anyone like him.
  He spoke quietly, his words were tender and kind.

I kept waiting for the moment his conversation would change.
  Instead, he listened to me, it was really strange.
  I confessed so much hurt to a stranger I didn't know.
  I guess my misery and despair
  had reached overflow.

He didn't judge me as I tried to explain
how I felt inside — all my hurt and pain.
Hours went by but it seemed only a moment.
I emptied my heart to this stranger and my torment
seemed less and less, I finally began to cry.

My voice became a whisper and turned into an inward sigh.
This stranger stayed near me, listened to my inner plea.
He became a friend that eventually set me free.
He returned to see me day after day.
His encouragement and acceptance helped me find my way.

He introduced me to God, I person I never knew,
I felt if God was like this man, he must be true.
He's no longer a stranger, this man and his God.
I am learning to live a life without fear.
I can whisper, I'm not afraid of what I might hear.  ↩

*How Can I Love?*

# Matthew ~·

I grew up in a good family, went to the best schools, obtained a good job in my profession, purchased a big house, had good friends and married my college sweetheart.

I had it all until the parties got too long and the drugs too strong. One day I awakened and my world was upside down. I am thirty-two.

## Ashes ~·

I woke up, looked around
    and wondered
        what to do.

Another day to
    search for
        something to hang on to.

My hands are shaking,
    my insides quaking,
        needing an instant fix.

I got to have something
    'cause I ain't nothing
        until I have my mix.

For one fleeting moment
    I thought about Momma
        and the dullness went away.

I need an answer
    to living —
        What is life anyway?

Thirty-two years
    I been on this earth.
        Must be a reason why.

So many unanswered questions —
    Is a man born
    just to die?

What a cruel hoax —
    millions of folks existing
        from day to day.

I want to believe
            there is a reason for it all
                        somehow or someway.

Something inside me cries,
            but the tears
                        never reach the surface.

I haven't cried since I was five,
            tears
                        don't have no purpose.

Only children cry
            and I am grown,
                        but all I feel is ache.
                                    Somebody — anybody...
                                    I need a break!

What is life?
            Life never gives,
                        it takes. ⌣

## Life ~·

I was so low, I had run aground.
Then John told me about this therapist he knew in town.
He said she could help, I needed to believe
because three months ago John was in my fix.

He's better now. His load has been lifted.
His face is bright, his luck has shifted.
John has a a job now, in his old profession
— he is a lawyer in a large corporation.

His act has changed. He's pretty straight.
I figured I'd try this therapist before it was too late.
I went and now I am glad I did.
She found all the secrets I thought I hid.

At first I couldn't believe the things she said to me.
After only a few visits I felt victory.
She touched the heart of my problems, as though she lived in my head.
She listened to my heart and not just what I said.

She understood the reason why sometimes I wanted to die.
She introduced me to my inner boy that needed to cry.
I lived in denial, self-pity and shame.
It was easy to always think of others to blame.

She said my failures were not failures at all,
but a warning to take a different path or fall.
I took a good look at me and my sojourn through life.
In my Journey there will always be some pain and strife.

She told me to look carefully for simple treasures overlooked.
She encouraged my transparence to be an open book.
It's all about Potential and Possibilities —
a daily search for who I can be.

I look at life a lot differently today.
I got some wise counsel that showed me the way.
My therapist gave me a copy of a poem she wrote.
When I begin slipping I begin to quote —

    I am a garden of potential
            I can plant anything —
    I can plant a see of memory
            and become a Historian
    I can plant a seed of truth
            and become a great Writer
    I can plant a seed of integrity
            and become a great president
    I can plant a seed of justice
            and become a great judge
    I can plant a seed of understanding
            and become a great teacher
    I can plant a seed of kindness
            and become a great Missionary
    I can plant a seed of gentleness
            and become a great protector of
            the rights of men and woman to be free —

I can be all these things because...
I have Great Potential and Possibility.

# How Can I Pray?

# Michelle ⌐·

My husband divorced me for a younger woman after twenty years of marriage. Since I have stayed home all these years where do I go from here? My friends don't seem to want me around anymore. Where will my support come from?

# Ashes ∿·

Here I am at the crossroads of life —
forty-five, single, bereft with strife.

Unemployed, lonely, no goals, no vision,
four children and hardly any provision.

My husband left me, after twenty-five
this was not my choice.

I sought job after job, heard the same
story in the same tone of voice,

"Sorry, no work experience, no resume,
no time to train."

Each time they communicate "you are not wanted,"
I writhe with pain.

I hear, "You are uneducated, too old, inexperienced,
a nothing."

I raised four beautiful children —
doesn't that count for something?

Where is God in this, I plead
in pain and sorrow.

Like friends He makes promises,
but count on me tomorrow.

Tomorrow never comes. I am let down.
No benefits or insurance.

I am a second class citizen, a
misfit with no self assurance.

I am tired of listening to
others who depend on God for security and protection.

I can't pray anymore, I am
stuck with no direction.

# Life 〜·

I went to the support group desperate
for direction and light.
The women welcomed me with
such open delight.

I was so surprised I could
hardly speak.
In fact, I didn't, I sat silent
in my seat.

As I listened to the women share
openly of their past,
it was all so different, their hardships
didn't last.

Like me, some were rejected and
left alone.
Together they gained the strength and
faith to overcome.

No problem was too difficult, no
circumstance too great.
These women believed that it
was never too late…

To discover the purpose that God
created us for.
I soon discovered hidden talents
as I began to explore.

With daily caution, I let
my barriers down.
And found out why my
faith had gone aground.

I dwelt too long on what I could not do,
so I began to thank God for what I like to do.

I like to sew, garden, grow roses, landscape,
make good food and draw.
I like to watch birds,
animals and see people smile.

I like flowers, the earth and sky,
I like to drive.
I like hostessing,
watching children play.

I am connected now. I believe
I can pray.

# About the Author

Dr. Phillips has been a consultant to numerous organizations throughout the United States, as well as a conference leader to national organizations and churches throughout the Northwest and other states.

As a child and family advocate, Dr. Phillips has been a crusader for the improvement of families and the rights of children to be reared in loving families. She and her husband founded Give Us This Day, Inc. in 1979, an agency that provides counseling, adoption, respite care and extended family homes. In June, 1994, Dr. Phillips started a reorganization of the agency to impact families and children nationally by introducing the National Extended Family Institute. She has won numerous awards over the years, including the prestigious Jefferson Award, the White Rose Award and the Clara M. Hale Humanitarian Award by the National Delta Sigma Theta Sorority.

Dr. Phillips is very sensitive to the hurts and pains of others, especially those who come to her for counseling. She is the mother of ten children and the grandmother of twenty-two. She has written children's stories for years as a legacy to her grandchildren and has published several children's books. Dr. Phillips is currently working on two books. The first covers a series of topics of interest to parents, educators and the general public regarding culturally sensitive issues called "Ask Ofidean." The second book chronicles twenty of her twenty-two grandchildren, highlighting comical incidents in their lives.

Dr. Phillips resides in Sherwood, Oregon with her husband Rev. Joshua D. Phillips, a family therapist.

# About the Illustrator

Rondahl A. Mitchell Phillips (Ron) began drawing at age three. Encouraged by Dr. Phillips, his style is one of boldness and vibrant use of color. He presently designs cards and publishes comics. The pen and ink illustrations presented in this volume are variations on a rose theme denoting life. Ron lives in Sherwood, Oregon with his wife Emmaly and his year old son Royce.